KIN

Leader

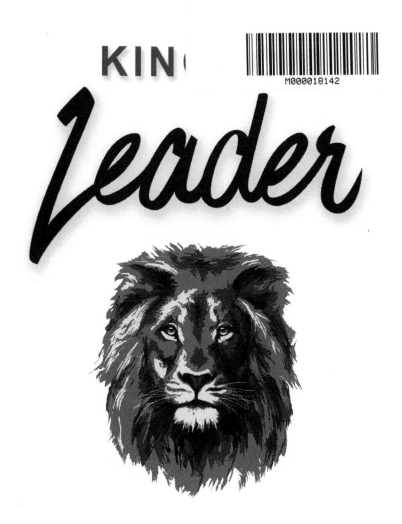

A 21 Day Journey To Unleash The Kingdom
Leader Within Us All

TAYLOR MORTON

Cover Design by 100Covers.com
Interior Design by FormattedBooks.com

In memory of my loving Mother-in-Law Loulee Williams Karn and two incredible students Anna Kamplain and Hudson Fife

CONTENTS

FOREWORD

God, in his infinite wisdom and perfection, created you with leadership potential and capacity. In fact, cultivating and stewarding influence is something that can be traced all the way back to the creation narrative, and thus is part of what it means to be made in the image of God. Mankind's sin and rebellion both distorts and cheapens how we view and approach the subject of leadership. Of course, redemption made possible by the finished work of Jesus Christ, makes it possible for us to again influence for God's glory. This is why Paul wrote, "For we are God's masterpiece. He has created us anew in Christ Jesus, so we can do the good things he planned for us long ago" (Ephesians 2:10).

Think about that one for a moment...YOU are GOD'S masterpiece!

Why?!?

so WE can do the good things HE planned for us long ago.

We are God's handiwork, a thing of his making, so we can accomplish the desires of God. Another way of looking at it is that until we became a thing of His making we couldn't accomplish the purposes of a people redeemed. Or as scholars have already written: "We are not *saved* by, but *created unto*, good works."[1]

This brings us to the subject of this incredible devotion written by my friend Taylor Morton: *to care about the good things God planned for us long ago is to care about becoming a 'Kingdom Leader'.* The following pages are written by a pastor, entrepreneur, practitioner, leader, athlete, husband, and now two-time author. In each role and with each platform I have personally witnessed Taylor seek to steward and maximize his influence to further God's kingdom. That is why I can say I am crazy-proud to see that spirit of intentionality spill out of his life and onto these pages.

Brent Crowe

1

Jamieson, R., Fausset, A. R., & Brown, D. (1997). Commentary Critical and Explanatory on the Whole Bible (Vol. 2, p. 345). Oak Harbor, WA: Logos Research Systems, Inc.

FOREWORD

Leadership. It means different things to different people. Some will want power, others want prestige, but followers of Christ want influence. Influence to change lives with the Gospel. The Apostle Paul experienced the power of God in his life. The power that made him a Kingdom Leader. As you walk through these 21 characteristics of a Kingdom Leader, learn from Paul. Understand he is writing from a prison cell. His life was unwavering. His life had been tried and tempted, challenged and attacked, but stayed true to the calling. Leaders do not quit if it gets tough or they are attacked. It is through the struggles and battles that your faith will become your "own" faith and not just something you've heard. It becomes who you are. Over these next 21 days, you will be challenged to live life outside the box of mediocrity. Taylor attacks head on the "just get by" attitude that destroys many potential leaders. I have personally watched Taylor live out these devotions that are in this incredible book. So, what is the opportunity ahead for you? It's the chance of a lifetime. To be unleashed to live for something bigger than yourself. For God to mold you into... well...a leader! Throughout these next 21 days, take this book personally. Don't try to put other people into the mental picture of the devotion. Allow these devotions to shape YOU. For over thirty years, I have seen leaders rise and fall. They rise by the hand of God. Why? Because God is always faithful to grant a platform for a leader. However, we must be the men and women who can handle the platform to be the leader that lasts. This means to be the men and women described in this book. I look forward to seeing what God will do in your life when you finish these next 21 days. You will not be finished by a long shot. You will though be heading in the right direction. D. L. Moody said over a hundred years ago, "the world has yet to see what God could do with one person who was totally surrendered to Christ." My prayer is that you may be that person! Come on...let's learn to live to be a Kingdom Leader!

Scott Dawson

PREFACE

The dictionary defines a *leader* as one that leads or guides. The word *lead* is defined as showing the way by going in advance. I like that. There is an old cliché that says "You can't lead where you haven't already been." I certainly believe that is not just a cliché. That it is a truth.

In our modern culture there is a great shortage of strong leadership. Or for that matter, leadership of any kind. Unfortunately, the failure to produce leaders has crept into the church specifically and into the Kingdom of God in general.

Beyond the fundamentals of salvation, God is calling everyone that claims the name of Jesus as Savior and Lord to be a leader. This call to be a leader is grounded in discipleship where one has to be steadfastly devoted to the study of, and obedience to, God's Word.

The age-old question is as follows: are leaders born or are leaders made? The answer is... yes! As believers, God uniquely gifts us all with gifts that are to be used for the advancement of the Kingdom. Regardless of how you view yourself, Jesus views you as chosen and uniquely qualified to lead others for His glory.

In *"Kingdom Leader,"* Taylor Morton has done an outstanding job of guiding the reader through what a Christian leader looks like. The twenty-one truths Taylor focuses on in this daily study guide are life transformational. You will be encouraged and challenged as you discover Biblica requirements for leadership well beyond your comfort zone.

Without a doubt, if you will spend three weeks in this study, you will experience a transformation only Jesus can produce as He begins to unleash the Kingdom leader within you.

Dr Billy Joy

INTRODUCTION

Kingdom Leader is a twenty-one-day devotional that takes you on a journey that strives to unleash the Kingdom leader inside of you. We will look at what the apostle Paul writes to the Church of Colossae in Colossians chapter three. In chapter one and two of Colossians, Paul focuses the majority of his letter on teaching the church theology, but in chapter three he then turns his focus towards applying the theology he taught in the earlier chapters. He taught the church of Colossae how to be a new creation, and he taught them how to be Kingdom leaders. We are going to dive into what it looks like to be a Kingdom leader, in a culture that is so consumed with this world. This devotional was written to encourage believers to rise up and be the leader that God created them to be. Before we start this journey, you need to understand the meaning behind the journey lasting twenty-one days. It takes twenty-one days to develop a habit, and this devotional's intent is for you to get into the habit of becoming a Kingdom leader. Not just for twenty-one days, but the rest of your life. What will you do for the glory of God? How will you make a difference for the Kingdom? Make today count. There's no time to wait. Unleash the Kingdom leader within! Dr. Jay Strack once said, "Leaders aren't made in a day, but they are made daily." Let's start the daily process of becoming a Kingdom leader.

Taylor Morton

DAY 1

A Leader's Heart

> *Colossians 3:1*
> *Since then you have been raised with Christ, set your*
> *hearts on things above where Christ is at the right*
> *hand of God.*

One of the most dynamic elements of a leader is the leader's heart. The heart is the center of who you are as a leader. When you focus on the word "heart," what comes to your mind? I ask this question whenever I preach on Colossians three, and whenever I ask this question, the response is typically something like: "love," "Valentine's Day," or something of that nature. The heart represents love, but it also represents our passions and our desires.

Paul urges us in Colossians 3:1 to set our hearts (passions) on things above, as he refers to things above he is referring to the Kingdom of God.

The question we must ask ourselves is: Are our passions and desires set on the Kingdom? My top three passions that come to my mind, when I think about the question, are my marriage, speaking, and football. Those are three of my passions. I love my wife. I also have a fire in my heart for speaking. It is one of my favorite things to do. And at one point in my life, I loved playing the game of football. So, what would these passions and desires look like if I transformed these passions and desires from just my marriage, speaking, and football to Kingdom passions and desires? Instead of just being married, my marriage would be a marriage that pointed to Jesus. Instead of just speaking, I would be preaching the Gospel. Instead of just playing a game called football, I would be playing football for the glory of God.

When our hearts are set on the Kingdom, our passions become eternal instead of a passion that just withers away. Mark 8:36 says *"For what does it profit a man to gain the whole world and forfeit his soul?"* This world is going to pass away, but our relationship with Jesus Christ will last forever. It is time we transform our passions and desires into something that will last forever. If we are going to be leaders for the Kingdom, it starts with our heart.

List your top three passions:

_____

_____

_____

Now how can you transform those passions into "Kingdom Passions"?

_____

_____

_____

_____

_____

_____

Additional Notes:

_____

_____

_____

_____

_____

_____

_____

PRAYER

Lord, may my heart be set on you and may my passions and desires bring glory to your name. Amen.

Day 2

A Leader's Focus

Colossians 3:2
Set your minds on things above, not on earthly things.

The focus of the leader typically makes the heart of the leader. What your focus is on so your heart will be on also. Garbage in means garbage out. What you fill your mind with is molding your mind. You can either choose to fill it with Kingdom things or worldly things. One of those things brings life, and the other brings destruction. Focusing is hard to do for many people, including myself; I have ADDDDDHDHDDDDDD. I went and was tested back in 2014 to see what my results were. It was very apparent that I was not only ADHD, but I had tested in the ninety eighth percentile.

What causes us to lose focus? Distractions and lack of discipline are two things that can cause us to lose focus. The world wants to take our focus off the kingdom. John 10:10 reminds us that *"the thief comes to kill steal and destroy."* Satan would love nothing more than to get your focus off what God has in store for you. Satan wants to distract you with the things of this world that look so appealing, so that he can kill, steal, and destroy you. The simplest example I can think of on focus is a horse. When I was a young boy, my Nana would take my two brothers and me to the Montevallo Christmas parade. This was something that we looked forward to every single year. I was always amazed at how the horses that carried the carriages stayed the course. They did not get distracted. The reason being is that the horses wore blinders beside their eyes to help them stay the course.

We need to put on blinders for the things that distract us from the Kingdom. Those blinders are put on for us by spending time in God's Word, by spending time in prayer, and by surrounding ourselves with a body of believers that are there to encourage us and hold us accountable. The mind is such a valuable and fragile thing. Protect it with your focus. May your focus be on the Kingdom.

List three things that are knocking you off cou

_____

_____

_____

Spend time in God's word this week. Set aside a specific time each day for prayer. If you are not plugged into a local body of believers get connected!

Additional Notes:

_____

_____

_____

_____

_____

_____

PRAYER

Lord, protect my mind so that it will be focused on you. May my mind be Kingdom focused for your glory. Amen.

A Leader's Identity

> Colossians 3:3
> *For you died, and your life is now hidden with Christ in God*

In 2017, the United States was hit with its largest cyber security breach. Over half of our population was affected when Equifax was hacked into. In our day and age, we are constantly at risk of having our identity stolen by hackers and identity thieves. There is a constant battle to try and protect our identities through cyber security agents and different companies that offer services to try and help protect your identity.

There is also a spiritual battle going on every single day for your identity. John 10:10 states that *"the thief comes to kill, steal, and destroy."* The enemy (Satan) wants to steal our identity. Our identity is found in Christ, but every single day the enemy tries to convince us otherwise. In Colossians 3:3, Paul tells us that our old identity is dead. This dead identity is the one that the enemy keeps trying to resuscitate, by telling us that the world has so much to offer. This world is going to pass away. What this world has to offer is only temporary, but where our true identity is found lasts forever. That identity is found in Jesus Christ. We need to stop living like our old self, but start living in the new self that God intended us to be.

As a child, I remember falling down and scraping my knee a bazillion times. Whenever I would scrape my knee, it would always scab over, and like every other kid down the street, I would pick at the scab until it was healed. Once it was healed, there was a piece of new skin there where the old skin had fallen off. When we peeled the scab, we did not try to stick it back on, but we got rid of it and were done with it.

A kingdom leader leaves the past in the past and moves forward. We look to the past for guidance, but we do not cleave to it. We live in the new identity that Christ has called us to. Whatever you're holding onto, let it go - throw the scab away and let the skin heal. Press on!

What are the scabs you need to get rid of?

_____

_____

_____

Additional Notes:

_____

_____

_____

_____

_____

_____

PRAYER

Lord, remind me who I am in you. Help me to die to my flesh daily so that in all things may I glorify you. Amen.

Day 4

A Leader's Life

When something is your "life," that "something" consumes who you are. Some would say, that "something" would be your "god." In the state of Alabama, it is either Alabama football is your "life" or Auburn football is your "life." Those two teams consume people in this state. On any given Saturday, there will be over 100,000 people in a stadium worshipping a football team. I love what Rick Burgess says about the game of football, he says "football is a great game, but a terrible god." When you claim something is your life, you are essentially claiming that thing is your god. Well, when Paul is stating that Christ is our "life," he is stating that Christ is our God. Are we living like Christ is our life? Matthew 6:33 says *"seek ye first the Kingdom of God and all these things will be added to you as well."* Christ being our life is all about putting Jesus first in everything that we do.

As leaders, we tend to get caught up on projects and agendas. Neither of the two are bad, but when they become our life and take the place of Christ, we have fallen into the enemy's trap. Keep Christ first in everything you do. Stop compartmentalizing your relationship with Him. Stop walking out of the church doors and leaving faith on the pew. Carry it with you every single day in every aspect of your life. How we live our lives is worship. Live in a way that says my life is all about Christ and not about anything other than Him. As a Kingdom leader, we must keep Him first.

List your top 5 priorities: (be honest)

1)_____

2)_____

3)_____

4)_____

5)_____

What do you need to do to make sure that Christ is number one in your life? What is taking His place in your life?

_____

_____

_____

_____

_____

_____

Additional Notes:

_____

_____

_____

_____

_____

_____

PRAYER

Lord, help me to prioritize my life according to your will. Whatever stands in the way of your position in my life help me to eliminate that accordingly. Amen.

Day 5

A Leader's Character

> Colossians 3:5-6
> *Put to death, therefore, whatever belongs to your earthly nature: sexual immorality, impurity, lust, evil desires and greed, which is idolatry. Because of these God's wrath is coming.*

It takes forever to create a reputation, and one moment to destroy it all. As leaders, we must daily build our character. Our character is built by what is done in our private life. Dr. Brent Crowe says it best when he says, "whatever is done in the dark will be revealed in the light." Who you are when no one else is looking will be revealed at some point in time, and you cannot hide who you really are.

As a leader, our character is everything. We must put to death the things that are of our flesh, as listed in Colossians 3:5. If those things linger in our lives, then at some point they will be brought to light. One of my favorite leaders and mentors is Dr. Jay Strack. I love SLU, SLU stands for *Student Leadership University*; without SLU, I would not be where I am at today. At SLU 101, I remember Dr. Jay sharing a story about toothpaste. He was speaking to the Tampa Bay Buccaneers, and he went around asking the players as he is holding a tube of toothpaste: "What will come out when I squeeze this tube?" All of the players, of course, answered, "white tooth paste" that was what was expected because that is what it looked like. Well, what the players did not know was that Dr. Jay had replaced the tooth paste with hot sauce, and when he squeezed the tube, red hot sauce came out. Well, of course, the players were blown away by the fact that red hot sauce came out instead of white tooth paste. What Dr. Jay was pointing out to the Buccaneers was that who you are will be revealed when you are squeezed. When life gets tough and when you get "squeezed" in life, who you are eventually comes out.

What you do in the quiet hours will be revealed when the light comes on. As a former football player, what I did at practice would be revealed during the game. Developing our character as leaders is so essential. We must not take part in any of the devious acts mentioned in Colossians 3:5; those must be put to death so they will never be shown in the light. When we are squeezed, the you that comes out will be the you that is leading for the Kingdom of God. Die to your flesh and live for Jesus daily; it's worth it!

If and when you are squeezed what will come out of you?

_____

_____

_____

_____

_____

_____

Additional Notes:

_____

_____

_____

_____

_____

_____

_____

PRAYER

Lord, give me the strength to put to death the things of my flesh that hinder me from being all that I can be for your glory. Amen.

Day 6

A Leader's Past

> *Colossians 3:7-8*
> *You used to walk in these ways, in the life you once lived. But now you must also rid yourselves of all such things as these: anger, rage, malice, slander, and filthy language from your lips.*

Your past does not define who you are, but it sure does create a great learning opportunity. Paul states that we used to walk in "these" ways. We "used to" is important, which does not mean we continue to. Our past serves a purpose, and that purpose is to learn, not always to replicate. If you are trying to create change in your life and you continue to do the same thing, that is the definition of insanity. If you are trying to remove filthy language from your lips but you continue to surround yourself with people who are always using vulgar language, you will probably continue down that track.

You are who you hangout with. At some point, it has to click for us. Scripture is very clear: scripture tells us if you love me you'll obey my commands. If we truly know Jesus and if we truly love Jesus, we will obey His commands. We will truly start living for him. This does not mean that we totally neglect or forget our past, but we learn from it. I was listening to a podcast where Louie Giglio was talking about sin, and he said it so brilliantly. He said that obviously we'll never be to the point where we are sinless. We live in a fallen creation so obviously there is still going to be sin in our life, but what we can do is we can "sin- less."Most of us hold on to our past or regret it so much that it bears us down, and the weight is way too much to carry. When I think about the past and sometimes the burden that it brings, it reminds me of a picture Kyle Creel took while in Tampa. Kyle was driving back to Tuscaloosa, Alabama when he saw a car and in the car's trunk was a motorcycle. When he first saw the car, he wanted to laugh, but then began to realize that many times, we are like that car. We carry things around that God never intended us to. To be a great leader we must learn from the past, and anything in our past that holds us back from being the very best we can be for Jesus we must let die.

Let the past die, and remember that your past does not define who you are.

Take a sheet of paper and write down the things of your past that is a continuous burden. Ball it up and throw it in the trash, because that is no longer who you are.

Additional Notes:

_____

_____

_____

_____

_____

_____

_____

PRAYER

*Lord, remind me who I am in you.
You call me blameless and you have
forgiven me. Remind me that I am a
child of God.
Amen.*

Day 7

A Leader's Routine

Colossians 3:9-10
Do not lie to each other, since you have taken off your old self with its practices and have put on the new self, which is being renewed in knowledge in the image of its Creator.

Unfortunately, routines get a bad reputation in the church. I've heard it said several times "be careful not to get into a routine." A routine of checking out while at church or a routine of being comfortable at church can be bad, and we must do everything we can to avoid that. The routine that makes us anything less than what God has called us to be can be devastating, but let's look at this from a totally different angle.

What if our routines glorified Christ? What if our routines prepared us to take on the day? What if our routines helped us to be an effective believer? Most people's routines are surrounded by the idea of how can I just get by. Let's transform that mindset into how can I create a daily routine that helps us to make the biggest impact while we are here on earth. Verse nine of Colossians three reveals that we are done with our old self. This means that we are done with our old routines and now we have put on the new self, which is being renewed in knowledge of the image of the Creator. This creates what I like to call power routines. If we are renewing something, that means we are constantly doing something. This constant renewal of our minds means that we are doing something daily to morph our mind into a mind that is focused on the Kingdom. That routine could be something as simple as spending time in God's Word daily. That is a routine that can transform our lives. Challenge yourself to create power routines that renew your mind daily. Create a power routine that makes you more effective as a believer. Routines are not a bad thing; they can be one of the most powerful things that transforms your life for the Kingdom.

Take a moment and circle three to five potential power routines that you can commit to. Pick three that will suit you and make you a more effective believer.

Power Routines:

Daily Bible Reading | Daily Book Reading | Daily Meditation | Workout | Scripture Memorization | Plan Your Week | Prayer

* These are all power routines. If you have a power routine that is not listed please share it with us at taylor-morton.net

Additional Notes:

_____

_____

_____

_____

_____

_____

_____

PRAYER

Lord, help me to create routines that honor and glorify you. Amen.

Day 8

A Leader's Diversity

> *Colossians 3:11*
> *Here there is no Gentile or Jew, circumcised or uncircumcised, barbarian, Scythian, slave or free, but Christ is all, and is in all.*

It was unheard of during the time that Paul wrote Colossians for Gentiles and Jews to associate. I think back to when Jesus took a short cut and ran into a Samaritan woman. Despite the unbelief of the disciples to what Jesus was doing, he still met with her. He knew how different she was. He knew that she had five husbands. He also knew that the man she was with now was not her husband. He still went to her and offered salvation.

Jesus shows a great leadership principle here: He shows His heart for diversity. His heart is for everyone. No matter if you're a Jew or a Gentile. No matter if you are slave or free Jesus loves you all the same.

As a leader for the Kingdom, we must view people from the lens of Jesus - with a heart full of diversity. Back in 2011, I was a senior in high school, and God laid on my heart to start a ministry called Converge. Converge Ministries vision was and is to break down racial, social, and denominational barriers that hinder the body of Christ from coming together to worship the one true and living God. As believers, we must break down any barrier that can hinder our expansion of our influence. No matter what ethnicity, no matter what social status, or no matter what financial status someone has, we must view them as Jesus would.

A true Kingdom leader sees one race - the human race. The true Kingdom leader sees only one social status - the opportunity to engage in conversation. The true Kingdom leader sees one financial status - that the money we have is only money that God let us borrow. What are we doing with that money to further His Kingdom? A true leader is diverse. He or she has a heart for diversity, but in that diversity, they seek to bring all together for the one true and living God.

Who are people that are different than you that you have a hard time being around?

_____

_____

_____

_____

_____

_____

How can you seek to bring them into your friend group or church?

_____

_____

_____

_____

_____

_____

_____

Additional Notes:

_____

_____

_____

_____

_____

PRAYER

Lord, help me to see all people - even people that are different than me - as Your children made in Your image. Give me the boldness to step out of my comfort zone and to engage with someone who is different. Amen.

Day 9

A Leader's Fruit

> Colossians 3:12
> *Therefore, as God's chosen people, holy and dearly loved, clothe yourselves with compassions, kindness, humility, gentleness and patience.*

Matthew 7:16 states, *"You will know them by their fruits."* Here in Matthew, Jesus is warning about false prophets. He warns them that you'll know them by their fruits. Jesus describes how a good tree produces good fruit and a bad tree produces bad fruit. As simple as that is, the principle is very insightful. You'll know a true believer by the fruit they produce, by the life that they live.

If you are a leader for the kingdom, you'll be producing fruit of compassion, kindness, humility, gentleness, and patience. The compassion that you have for people will extend past just the people you are close with because you will have a heart for all people. You will have a heart to serve people. Dr, Jay and Dr. Brent Crowe say it best when they say, "Leadership starts at the feet of Jesus." With leadership starting at the feet of Jesus, the leader has the heart of a servant. A heart that is willing to go the extra mile and serve others. Secondly, the fruit of kindness. Literally, this is being intentional about being kind to others. I want to challenge you to do three kind things today. Buy the person's lunch in the car behind you at the drive-thru. Sit by the student at lunch that no one speaks to. Call or text a friend or co-worker you know is struggling. Let them know that you are praying for them. Do not get so caught up in receiving blessing that you forget to be a blessing to someone today. Do not forget to be humble. Have a spirit of humility. People get the word humility confused. Humility is not putting yourself down, but humility is all about lifting others up. Be the biggest encourager in the room. Next, be gentle. Walk in a way that is not intimidating. Walk in a way that you are approachable. Be the person that someone can count on. Be the shoulder that someone can cry on. Have a gentleness about you that attracts and points people to Jesus. Lastly, be patient. When your boss is irritable and seems to always have something rude to say to you, pause for a moment, take a deep breath, and try to think about what he or she may be going through. Pray for them. Encourage them. When your waiter or waitress just cannot seem to bring you the "exact" thing you ordered, take a chill pill and realize that this maybe an opportunity God has placed in front of you to be His hands and feet and produce the fruit that a Kingdom leader should.

What are some random acts of kindness I can put into action today?

_____

_____

_____

_____

_____

_____

_____

Write down the people you need to be more patient with. The people that you need to show more compassion for.

_____

_____

_____

_____

_____

_____

Additional Notes:

_____

_____

_____

_____

_____

_____

_____

PRAYER

Lord, help me to be a leader that produces good fruit. Help me to show compassion to the people that You created in Your image. Help me to show kindness to those You have intentionally placed in my life. Teach me how to be humble and how to be patient and realize that everything has a purpose that is greater than I can comprehend. Amen.

Day 10

A Leader's Willingness to Forgive

> *Colossians 3:13*
> *Bear with each other and forgive one another if anyone has a grievance against someone.*

One of my favorite stories of forgiveness, besides the story of Jesus, is the story of Esau and Jacob. Jacob was so afraid that Esau was not going to forgive him for stealing his birthright and his blessing, but when Esau and Jacob finally met back again several years after this had happened, Esau ran to him and forgave him with no stipulations. He forgave Jacob, and the forgiveness Esau showed Jacob did several things. Number one, Esau forgave without any expectations. In Genesis 33:9, Esau says, *"I have enough, my brother; keep what you have for yourself."* Esau was content in what he had. If we are ever going to be a leader who has the heart to forgive, we must be content in what we have. Do not envy anything or anyone. Contentment not only expects nothing from anyone else, but it demands excellence in our own lives. If we walk around with the attitude of someone "owes" us something, then we will never get anywhere. We will always be at a stand still. If you want to be a leader, go earn it. Do not "expect it," If you want that position at work, go earn it. Don't complain about what you do not have. If you want that position on your sports team, don't make your parents go and sit down and talk with the coach, put your big boy and big girl pants on and go earn that spot. Be content and expect nothing. Forgive unconditionally. The second thing that happened, that was pretty awesome, was that through Esau forgiving Jacob, his forgiveness pointed Jacob to Jesus. In Genesis 33:10, it says, *"And Jacob said, 'No please, if I have now found favor in your sight then receive my present from my hand, inasmuch as I have seen your face as though I had seen the face of God, and you were pleased with me.'"* When we forgive, we are pointing people to Jesus. Jacob saw the face of God through Esau's forgiveness. When we forgive the people in our lives who have done us so much harm, the only answer that seems to make any sense is Jesus. Only a Kingdom Leader could forgive someone when they had stolen something from them as important as their birthright and their blessing, but because of Jesus, we can forgive the unforgivable and change the world. Lastly, a Kingdom leader lets the past die. Genesis 33:12 says *"Then Esau said, 'Let us take our journey; let us go, and I will go before you.'"* Let's move on. When we truly let the past die, we hold nothing else against the person who has wronged us. Everyone can move forward for the better. True forgiveness requires contentment. True forgiveness points people to Jesus. True forgiveness moves on.

Who do you need to forgive?

_____

_____

_____

Do the people you need to forgive have a relationship with Jesus?

_____

_____

_____

If not , where do you need to start with the evangelism process?

_____

_____

_____

Talk to your youth pastor or pastor about how to share the Gospel with your lost friends that you need to forgive.

Additional Notes:

_____

_____

_____

_____

_____

_____

_____

PRAYER

Lord, forgive me for when I fail you. Lord, help me to forgive as You forgave me.

Day 11

A Leader's Unifying Ability

Colossians 3:14
And over all these virtues put on love, which binds
them all together in perfect unity.

Unity is the act of coming together. When unity comes to mind, I immediately think of the Olympic games. The entire world comes together to compete. Stadiums fill, sponsorships are sold, and an alliance is formed. What brings all of these factors together? Love for country, money, star athletes, and a simple love for competitions. So, what brings the people God has put into your life together? God has placed people in your life to unify - to unify around the Gospel. Think for a moment what has brought your church family together. In December of 2017, I was serving as the student pastor at Valley View Baptist Church in Tuscaloosa, Alabama. I had only been at Valley View for two months when the unimaginable occurred. A student in my youth ministry by the name of Anna Kamplain experienced something that would rock our student ministry to its core. Anna was a brilliant and loving ninth grade girl. A word that defined her was the word: "Joy." Anna had recently undergone a liver transplant surgery, and with that surgery, came great hope. Eleven days after the transplant, Anna was being discharged from the hospital. She and her parents were in the elevator headed to get in the car to go home when Anna became very weak and fainted. At this point, she was taken back to her room to be evaluated. Ultimately, Anna was moved to ICU during the night while her medical team tried to figure out what was going on. Later the next day, Anna was taken back to the operating room, and she passed away later that evening. This sent shock waves through our entire student ministry and our church. Students and parents alike were all grieving. Anna's funeral was packed. Over a thousand people filled our worship center to pay their respects for Anna. Our student ministry decided to do a memorial service for her as well. This service brought students from every background and race together. Students challenged one another, students were encouraged by the Gospel, and students were inspired by the legacy Anna left. Trage-dy brought the students together that night but love for Anna and for Jesus bound them together. Anna would unify a room the moment she walked in. Her very pres-ence would do so. She radiated the love of God through every aspect of her life. Have joy like Anna.

Be a leader of unity. If you are trying to be a leader and you cannot bring people together, start with love. Love God, and love people. Love God with all of your heart! Love people as you love yourself. Put others first. Before you show people how much you know, you must show them how much you care. A leader knows the impor-tance of unity. They realize that we are stronger together. A leader's unifying ability will depend on "buy-in" of the people that God has placed in your life. As a leader if you do not have "buy-in," you have probably lost the ability to lead that particular group. Check yourself. Make sure you put others before yourself. When I was playing high school football and even in college, I would walk into the locker room and there would be signs everywhere. These signs would have sayings on them. For instance, at Alabama, one sign that I saw every single day was a sign that said "effort." When you left the locker room for practice that day, you would think about effort. The ef-fort that you would put forth in the practice or game that day. A sign that I distinctly remember from back in high school was a sign that had the phrase on it that read: "TEAM is greater than ME." That is the mindset we must have as a leader. Others before me, and that starts with a heart of love for others. Love God. Love People.

How can you put someone else above yourself today?

_____

_____

_____

_____

Who do you need to pray for today?

_____

_____

_____

_____

_____

List three people that you can make a difference in their life today by finding a simple way to serve them.

1) _____

2) _____

3) _____

Additional Notes:

_____

_____

_____

_____

_____

_____

_____

PRAYER

*Lord, help me to love people the way
that You love them.*

Day 12

A Leader's Peace-Making Ability

> *Colossians 3:15*
> *Let the peace of Christ rule in your hearts, since as members of one body you were called to peace and be thankful.*

If you watch any news outlet today, there is always tension. Someone is always ready to fight someone else's point of view. People tend to show everyone what they are against, but no one can show people what they are for. A leader must be willing to bridge gaps unify and bring peace. If your first thought about someone is negative, your peace-making ability is way below where it needs to be. A leader gives everyone they come in contact with an opportunity. Regardless of race, religion, or socioeconomic status, they give them a chance. The first thought is always positive. Paul encourages us to let the peace of Christ rule in our hearts. If peace is going to rule in our lives, positive thinking has to be a priority. Serving enthusiastically has to become a part of who we are. Seeing others the way that God sees people is how our vision has to change. I have worked in several churches. Whether it be a big church or a small church, there is always that one person who I like to call a pot stirrer. A pot stirrer is someone who is always looking for something to talk about. A pot stirrer will make up something about someone just to create a conversation. A pot stirrer finds joy in talking behind someone's back. Don't be a pot stirrer. Be a peace keeper. Do not get excited one someone else fails, but instead, help them to get back up. Be the biggest encourager in the room, and get excited when others have success. That is the mark of a true leader.

Who do you need to reach out to and apologize to for stabbing in the back?

_____

_____

_____

_____

Write a list of pot stirrers you need to stop spending so much time with:

1) _____

2) _____

3) _____

Additional Notes:

_____

_____

_____

_____

_____

_____

_____

PRAYER

Lord, help me to not be a pot stirrer. Help me to glorify you with my actions towards all people. Train my mind to have a positive attitude.

Day 13

A Leader's Thirst for God's Word

Colossians 3:16
Let the word of Christ dwell richly among you, in
all wisdom teaching and admonishing one another
through psalms, hymns, and spiritual songs, singing
to God with gratitude in your hearts.

A leader for the Kingdom makes the Bible a big deal. Two of my favorite people in the entire state of Georgia are Chuck Allen and Tripp Atkinson. Chuck is the pastor at Sugar Hill Church, and Tripp is the student pastor. They are doing incredible things for the Kingdom of God in the city of Sugar Hill that is spreading throughout the globe. The mission of their church is this: "They believe the Bible is a big deal, and they believe that Jesus is the biggest deal of all." Their mission is what every leader must make their mission in their heart. They need to make the Word of God a big deal in their life, and they need to make Jesus an even bigger deal. When leader's make the Bible and Jesus a big deal in their lives, others follow. Others do the same. In verse sixteen, Paul encourages the church to teach and admonish one another. The way we teach one another and admonish one another is by knowing God's Word. The only way to know it is to spend time in his Word. Reading something and knowing something are two totally different things. When I arrived on campus at the University of Alabama, I was given a defense play-book that seemed to be over 500 pages long. I could read it all day long, but if I did not know the play-book, it was not going to benefit me at all in practice. I would be running around aimlessly on the practice field making a fool of myself. When you know the play-book, everything becomes second nature. You do not even have to think, and you react when things happen because you are well prepared. When you know God's Word, your reactions are completely different than they are when you are just reading the Bible to check a box. Allow God's Word to be a big deal in your life so that you can make a difference for the Kingdom and so that you can know your creator more each day.

When is the last time you made your quiet time with God a priority?

_____

_____

_____

_____

What is the last scripture you've memorized? Don't say John 3:16.

_____

_____

_____

_____

_____

_____

_____

Pick a verse each week to memorize for the remainder of this month. Allow God's word to become a part of who you are. See Psalm 119:11.

_____

_____

_____

_____

_____

Additional Notes:

_____

_____

_____

_____

_____

_____

_____

PRAYER

Lord, give me a thirst for Your Word. Guide me as I study it. Help me to apply Your Word to every aspect of my life.

Day 14

A Leader's Action

Colossians 3:17
And whatever you do, whether in word or deed, do it all in the name of the Lord Jesus, giving thanks to God the Father through him.

It's not always about what you do, but it is about why you do it and how you do it. When you go for a check-up and you meet with your doctor, you discover that he tells you that you are going to have to undergo surgery. The "why" in why that physician is practicing medicine will determine your state of comfort while undergoing the procedure. If you find out that the physician is simply just practicing medicine for the financial benefits, then that may lead you to have some discomfort before your procedure, but if you know the doctor's heart and the doctor's "why" for practicing medicine is to truly help people and that the physician has a heart for serving people and seeing people get physically better, then the way you feel about the physician operating on you changes. The way you feel then has more comfort, and it's because you trust the "why" in which the physician is operating. Our "why" should be one of the most important things about us as leaders. As Kingdom leaders, our "why" is not defined in anything from this world, but our "why" is defined in our purpose from Christ. We do as Paul encourages the Colossians to do, and that is to do everything in the name of the Lord Jesus. Our "why" is bigger than us, because our "why" is eternal. It is a heart and a mind shift. When we set our hearts on things above and when we focus our minds on things above, our "why" starts to transform into a "Kingdom" why. The goal for a Kingdom leaders' "why" should be to stop compartmentalizing their relationship with Christ but to look at every situation through a Christ first lens. For example, one afternoon my friend Evan and I went to Family Dollar to pick up some $1 candy before we went to the movies. We occasionally will do that instead of paying $6 for candy at the movie theater. We racked up on Sour Patch Kids and Sour Gummy Worms, and we went to check-out. As we were checking out, an older lady interrupted our transaction by asking the cashier how much a can of Raviolis were. When she heard the amount, she said "Well, all I can afford is the

Cheese Its." I heard her, but I really wasn't paying attention to her and her needs because I was more consumed with trying to get our cheap candy and rush to the movie theater. I was more annoyed, than I was concerned, and I unfortunately let an opportunity to have a Christ first lens slip by. If I would have looked at that situation through a Christ first lens instead of a self-centered, movie loving candy addict lens then the situation might have gone a little differently. I would have simply told the lady to put both of her items on my transaction and checked out, but it wasn't Sunday or Wednesday and I did not have my church clothes on and I was not in my Valley View student pastor pull-over representing the church I serve. That's the compartmentalization that has to stop. It should not matter what day it is, who it is, or where we are; we should do everything as if we are serving the Lord and that includes checking out at Family Dollar. We should serve because we are a new creation, and Paul clearly tells the church of Colossae that our life is now hidden in Christ, so everything we do should reflect Him.

What is an example that you may have of where you missed an opportunity to have a "Christ first" lens?

_____

_____

_____

_____

_____

_____

_____

_____

How would have acted differently in that situation looking back with a "Christ first" lens?

_____

_____

_____

_____

_____

_____

What is an area of your life that you are compartmentalizing from your relationship with Christ?

_____

_____

_____

_____

_____

_____

Additional Notes:

_____

_____

_____

_____

_____

_____

_____

_____

PRAYER

Lord, help me to be all in for You in every aspect of my life. Help me to see every situation through Your eyes and not my own. Lord, forgive me for failing to see people and situations the way that You see them.

Day 15

A Leader in the Family

> *Colossians 3:18-21*
> *Wives submit yourselves to your husbands, as fitting in the Lord. Husbands, love your wives and do not be harsh with them. Children obey your parents in everything, for this pleases the Lord. Fathers do not embitter your children, or they will become discouraged.*

"As the family goes so goes the nation." These words were spoken so brilliantly at SLU 201 from Dr. Jay Strack. As our culture rapidly changes, the family continues to desecrate. Ten years ago, when I was a student coming through Centreville Baptist's student ministry, the family was broken, but there would be at least one parent in the picture. Today, the family is even more desecrated where the student is no longer living with either parent. The student maybe living with a grandmother, an aunt or uncle, or in the foster system. We are in a battle for the family. The result of the family desecrating is leading to an opioid epidemic, alcohol consuming minds, and homelessness becoming something that is becoming more normal. How do we save the family? Paul gives the Kingdom outline of what the family should look like. First, Paul addresses the wives. Wives play a crucial part in the family. The family is not one person; the family is made up of multiple people serving in different capacities. The wife plays are crucial role in the family. Paul writes that the wife is to submit to her husband, as it is fitting to the Lord. This text doesn't mean that the wife is to have blind obedience to her husband but to submit to the leadership if their leadership is consistent with how a Kingdom leader should live. In other words, be a great supporter. Be an encourager. I know I have mentioned SLU a lot in this devotional, but there are so many great truths that I have taken away from their organization. Dr. Jay tells students you might not be the smartest person in the room, you might not be the most athletic person in the room, but one thing you can be is the biggest encourager in the room. I would not just encourage wives and future wives to be big encouragers, but husbands to be big encouragers as well. I would tell husbands that your wife's dreams and goals matter too! Paul then tells husbands to love their wives and do not be harsh with them. God is calling husbands to love their wives as Christ loved the church. God is not calling men to rule over their wives as some dictator, but to serve their wives well. To put them first. To encourage them to be the very best wife they can be. To point their wives towards Christ. To lead their wives in such a way that would bring honor and glory to the Kingdom. This kind of husband and wife relationship can change a culture and can change a generation because eventually the husband and wives will become mothers and fathers. Paul tells parents to love their children and not to embitter them or exasperate them. Encourage them. Lead them; point them to Jesus. Paul tells children to obey their parents, and that obeying them pleases God. Regardless of where you fit in this category I think we all can become better husbands, better fathers, better wives, better mothers, better sons, and better daughters. Let's reclaim the family. Take back our nation and see what God can do through the family when we live out His model for it.

Write down a few characteristics that you believe God wants you to have as a husband or wife one day?

_____

_____

_____

_____

_____

_____

_____

_____

What kind of son or daughter are you? Are you disobedient? Are you pleasing God with how you treat your parents?

_____

_____

_____

_____

_____

_____

_____

_____

If you're currently married when is the last time you served your spouse and put his or her needs above yourself?

_____

_____

_____

_____

_____

_____

_____
_____
_____
_____

I challenge you to encourage your spouse, your parents or your children today! Be the biggest encourager in the room. What is one way you can encourage someone today?

_____
_____
_____
_____
_____
_____
_____
_____

Additional Notes:

_____
_____
_____
_____
_____
_____
_____
_____

PRAYER

Lord, I am not perfect, but I am trying. I want to be a part of the generation that takes back the family. Help me to be who you have called me to be. Help me to lead well and help me to be the biggest encourager in the room.

Day 16

A Leader's Servanthood

> *Colossians 3:22*
> *Slaves, obey your earthly masters in everything; and do it, not only when their eye is on you and to curry their favor, but with sincerity of heart and reverence for the Lord.*

The term "slave" in the biblical era meant something different than the term "slaves" means today. The term "slave" could have referred to someone who was working for someone to pay off a debt that they may owe, and in this context, this seems to be the use. Paul tells the "slave" to obey their earthly masters in everything. And to not just work hard and obey them when they're watching you, but to obey them at all times. As Kingdom leaders, we are called to a life of servanthood. It is the act of humility that separates a Kingdom leader from a simple worldly leader. Being humble is not about putting yourself down, but it is about lifting others up. Paul encourages those who are working for their master to do things the right way. Let's compare this to our daily situations. We are not slaves to earthly masters, but we do serve. We serve on sports teams, in the classroom, at a job site, and in many student ministries, and there are people that God has placed in an authoritative position in your life for a reason. God wants you to serve them well. God wants you to do the right thing even when no else is watching. In my time in high school, videoing practice was a new and upcoming thing. During the blistering hot summers and falls in Alabama, it was easy to take a play-off when the coach was not looking. Several of the guys would do that, and I am not going to lie I would do that occasionally. Until, one practice Coach Battles (my high school football coach) had a camera guy come up, sit in a metal tower, and start filming practice. At first, it was terrifying; we were afraid to take a play off or be lackadaisical during any part of practice. Well, after several weeks of having a camera man at practice, it was easy to forget that he was there, and it was easy to start taking plays off again because you think no one is watching. This was all fun and games until Coach Battles went and re-watched the film. After re-watching the film, he saw that several guys were taking plays off and not giving their all, and he decided that the next day all of us would pay the price for not giving a 100% when we thought no one was watching. That payment was several hundred up-downs and a few 110-yard sprints. The importance of giving 100% in football when no-one is watching is vital to the success of the team. The importance of being all-in in our walk with Christ even when no one is watching can be the difference between a life of despair and an abundant life for the Kingdom. What happens in the dark is ultimately revealed in the light. What happens when no one is watching is the real you. In those moments, your character is being developed. Everyone can put on a fake face and act like they've got it all together and that they don't mess up. I challenge you to be the same person that you are in front of hundreds as you are in front of the One. Although we think we may be alone, we are never alone if we have a relationship with Christ. God is omnipresent. He is with you in the darkest of moments, and when you start playing with stuff that plays for keeps and you think that it won't catch up to you, it will. Do the right thing even when no one is watching; be all that you can be for the Kingdom. Live a life of integrity in the dark so that when you're in the light you can radiate the glory of Christ even more. Serve the people that God has placed in authority over your life well not just to get an "Atta boy or an Atta girl" but because you have an impeccable standard of excellence that supersedes any worldly treasure that could come your way. You are a child of God. Live like it.

When is the last time that you lived in the dark what you proclaim in the light?

_____

_____

_____

_____

What are you doing in the dark that you need to deal with and need to get out of your life?

_____

_____

_____

_____

_____

Who are some authority figures in your life? How can you serve them well?

_____

_____

_____

_____

_____

_____

_____
_____
_____
_____

Additional Notes:

_____
_____
_____
_____
_____
_____
_____

PRAYER

Lord, help me to be the real me. Help me to be the same person that I am in the light as I am in the dark. In my moments of character building, help me to become more like You and not like the rest of the world. Guide me in my decision making. Give me a pure mind and a pure heart.

Day 17

A Leader's Integrity

Colossians 3:23
Whatever you do, work at it with all your heart, as
working for the Lord, not for human masters.

Integrity is the art of doing the right thing when no one is looking. Today's devotional really contrasts well with yesterday's devotional. To be a Kingdom leader, integrity is everything. Paul in verse 22 encourages slaves to obey their masters even when no one is looking. Paul then follows that verse with telling them to work for the Lord and not for human masters. That's our motivation for integrity that our true master is God. Regardless of who your coach is, who your teacher is, or who your boss is everything should be done with a heart of integrity because we are working for the Lord not for man. This makes finishing the drill at practice more important because we are no longer compartmentalizing our relationship with Christ our life reflects our relationship with Christ. How we conduct our self at practice, how we walk down the halls of our school, and how we perform at work are no longer about earthly measures or earthly treasures, but it is all about glorifying Christ through everything we do. This literally gives purpose to every single moment of our life. It now matters how we interact with a stranger in the grocery store. It matters how we respond when our boss tells us to do something that we are not fond of doing. It matters when we don't finish a drill because we decided to take a play off because we thought no one was looking. The standard of excellence is no longer found in pleasing a coach, a boss, or a teacher, but the standard of excellence is now found in glorifying the One who created us. Make every moment count. Be excellent in all things because you are performing for the audience of One. How does this change the way we go about things? How does this change the way we respond to our parents when they're simply trying to parent us? How does this change the way we conduct ourselves at practice, in the classroom, or at the work site? Be a kingdom leader and remember that everything you do has purpose and that everything you do is either honoring to God or displeasing to Him.

List some ways that you can display integrity to the audience of One?

_____

_____

_____

_____

_____

Who is someone in your life that replicates a life of integrity?

_____

_____

_____

_____

_____

Ask a friend to help keep you in check! We all need someone to help us our journey and to help us make the moments count!

Additional Notes:

_____

_____

_____

_____

_____

_____

_____

_____

_____

PRAYER

Lord, remind me that I am working for you and that everything I do has a purpose. I pray that I will glorify you in the moments You have so blessed me with.

Day 18

A Leader's Reward

Colossians 3:24-25
Since you know that you will receive an inheritance
from the Lord as a reward. It is the Lord Christ you
are serving. Anyone who does wrong will be repaid
for their wrongs, and there is no favoritism.

Rewards, I love senior awards day! You get to see what a group of high school students have accomplished. On April 1st, 2007, I lost my brother Trent in an ATV accident. He was fishing with a friend, went to cross a road, was hit by an SUV, and it killed him instantly. Trent was a believer praise God for that, but when he passed away, my parents did not want to just receive flowers they wanted to give back so they set up a scholarship fund in his name. Over the past decade, the Trent McDaniel Morton Scholarship Fund has given out over $100,000 to students all across the country. The awards are a great honor to several deserving high school seniors. We try our best to make the award something that will have an eternal impact and not just an earthly reward. A lot of times when we receive a reward it is simply an earthly reward that will pass away. Students who receive the scholarship are picked based off of prior accomplishments and what their goals are. We hope to give the scholarship to future Kingdom leaders who will make an impact for the Kingdom. Paul tells the church of Colossae that their inheritance is from the Lord, and not from any earthly source. The inheritance is eternal life; it is being in the presence of Jesus for all of eternity. Nothing else could ever compare. Scripture says that better is one day in Your courts than a thousand elsewhere. What an inheritance! It's better than any amount of money, land, or "toys" we could ever receive. Journey with the eternal in perspective. Remember that this life is just a vapor. We are here today and gone tomorrow. Make the moment count and live in the perspective of the eternity.

What's an award that you have received? How can you utilize that reward to make an impact for the Kingdom?

_____

_____

_____

_____

_____

_____

How can you live within the perspective of the eternal?

_____

_____

_____

_____

_____

_____

_____

Additional Notes:

_____

_____

_____

_____

_____

_____

_____

PRAYER

Thank you for the precious gift of life. Help me to live with the perspective of eternity. Help me to make the moments you have given me count and not focus so much on material things.

Day 19

A Leader's Resiliency

Philippians 3:13-14
Brothers and sisters, I do not consider myself yet to
have taken hold of it. But one thing I do: forgetting
what is behind and straining toward what is ahead,
I press on toward the goal to win the prize for which
God has called me heavenward in Christ Jesus.

When my brother Trent passed away, my family and I
grieved tremendously. He was twelve years old when he
stepped into eternity. After the funeral, my parents gave
me everything that was found in his pocket. He was a
little chunky so he had a Snickers bar (I would have had
a Twix). He loved to have air-soft pellet gun wars so he

had a pocket full of orange air-soft pellets (he was the Rambo of air-soft gun wars). But then, I was presented something that sits on my desk and I look at every day. It was card, and on that card, it had the scripture Philippians 3:13-14 on it along with the phrase, "Never, Never Quit." That phrase comes from Winston Churchill's famous speech when he screamed from the top of his lungs "Never give in. Never give in. Never, never, never – in nothing great or small, large or petty never give in." This was Churchill's address to Harrow School on October 29, 1941. Continue the process was his message. It echoes the words from Paul as he tells the Philippians to strain towards what is ahead and to press on! For me, this was extremely important. Paul was addressing the Philippians to press on during the journey of sanctification. Sanctification is a big word but so is the word Frappuccino and most of us spend $5.75 on that at least three days a week. Sanctification means to become more like Jesus. To not give up; the goal is to become more like Christ. Through the card that was found in my brother's pocket, I am reminded daily that it is too soon to quit. The act of sanctification is happening every single day. It is not a sprint but a marathon. Sanctification does not happen in a day, but it does happen daily. It's not going to be easy, but you must press on. Life will be difficult, there will be ups and downs, but consistency as a Kingdom Leader is essential to one's resiliency. So, how resilient are you? When one thing does not go your way do you slip back into old habits? Or do you continue the pursuit of sanctification to be more like Christ today than you were yesterday? Never, Never Quit!

What are some ways that you can continue the act of sanctification?

_____

_____

_____

_____

_____

_____

_____

_____

_____

Are you going through something that has you wanting to quit? If so what is it? Let us know so we can be praying for you! Submit it at taylormorton.net

_____

_____

_____

_____

_____

_____

_____

_____

Additional Notes:

_____

_____

_____

_____

_____

_____

_____

_____

PRAYER

Lord, help me to become more like you. Sanctify me daily. Help me to stay disciplined and committed to the process.

Day 20

A Leader Invests in Others

Philippians 2:3-4
Do nothing out of selfish ambition or vain conceit.
Rather in humility value others above yourselves.

It takes a team to achieve a dream. We have all heard that statement a multitude of times. If it takes a team to achieve a dream, then we must take care of those who are on our teams. One way to do that is to value others above ourselves to take care of other's needs first. The Christian life is a life called to selflessness not selfishness. If humility is about lifting others up, then serving team becomes more about "them" than "me." One way to serve a team well is to treat everyone like they're a ten. We tend to treat people a certain way by their zip-code, name brand clothes, or who their parents are. What if, for a moment, none of that mattered? It shouldn't in the first place, but if we sat that aside for a moment and treated everyone like a 10 regardless of any of those factors, how different would your team look? What kind of impact would you make in those individual's lives? They matter too, and you might be the reason that they make it "out" of whatever situation they're in. Another way to serve your team well is to celebrate victories. We do this by getting excited when others have success instead of getting jealous because something didn't go well for you but it went well for someone else. Find ways to serve your team. Serve your friends and your classmates because you will only be as successful as the people around you are. Jesus had all authority in heaven given unto Him, and what did he do? He washed His disciples' feet. He served them well. Power is not about what you can take, but it is about what you can give. Ask yourself this question: are the people that God has placed around me better because I'm there? Are you bringing light into the room or darkness?

What is one way you can serve the people that God has placed around you?

_____

_____

_____

_____

_____

_____

_____

_____

Why are you jealous of other's success?

_____

_____

_____

_____

_____

_____

_____

_____

_____

Do you put yourself first or do you put others first?

_____

_____

_____

_____

_____

_____

_____

_____

What is one way you can celebrate an accomplishment of a friend, family member or co-worker?

_____

_____

_____

_____

_____

_____

_____

_____

Additional Notes:

_____

_____

_____

_____

_____

_____

_____

PRAYER

Help me to put You first and help me to love people the way that You do. Help me to realize it's not about me. Help me to have a team is greater than me mentality and help me to serve others well.

Day 21

A Leader Finishes Well

> *2 Timothy 4:7*
> *I have fought the good fight, I have finished the race,*
> *I have kept the faith.*

Paul was facing death, was coming towards the end of his ministry, and was facing impending martyrdom. His words to Timothy during his second Roman imprisonment were "I have fought the good fight, I have finished the race, I have kept the faith." In other words, "I have finished well." Of course, Paul made mistakes, but he strived every day to live a life that would glorify God. He was a Kingdom Leader. He led well. In Romans 12:1, he urges fellow brothers and sisters in Christ to be living sacrifices for the Kingdom. He urged them to be all-in. The difference between winning a national championship and coming in second place is finishing well. In 2013, we were playing Notre Dame in the Orange Bowl national championship game. The score at half time was 24-0. We came in the locker-room cheering as if we had already won the game. Coach Saban came in shortly after us and reminded us that we still had thirty minutes of football left to play in a way that only Coach Saban could. Coach understood the importance of finishing well. He understood that it was not about the score board, but it was about the standard of excellence in which we conducted ourselves through all four quarter of the game. It is important for us to finish well and to have a high standard of excellence in the way in which we live. In all four quarters of our life, we must have a high standard of excellence. Not just the moments at church camp or at church on Sunday or Wednesday but in every moment of our lives, Kingdom leaders pursue excellence. They live with a high standard of excellence regardless of where they are or who they are with because they realize that the moments they have been given have not been given to them for themselves but to glorify the one true and living God. When you get to the end of your life will you be able to say: "I have fought the good fight, I have finished the race, I have kept the faith?" It's important to start well, to fight well, and obviously to finish well.

After completing this 21-day journey, what has changed in you? Are you different or did you stay the same?

_____

_____

_____

_____

_____

_____

_____

_____

_____

_____

_____

_____

_____

_____

_____

_____

_____

_____

_____

_____

_____

_____

_____

_____

_____

_____

What are some ways you can finish well?

_____

_____

_____

_____

_____

_____

_____

Who are some examples of people in your life who have finished well?

_____

_____

_____

_____

_____

_____

_____

_____

Additional Notes:

_____

_____

_____

_____

_____

_____

_____

_____

_____

PRAYER

Lord, help me to be the Kingdom Leader you have created me to be. Help me to finish well and not get lazy during the routine of life. Every part of me belongs to You and You alone. Use me to make an impact for your Kingdom and to make an eternal mark.

CONCLUSION

A Kingdom leader lives a life that is surrendered to Jesus, takes the time to lead others, and changes the world. As you conclude this 21-day journey, my hope and prayer for you is that you would be that kind of leader. God has rescued you by His grace, gifted you with talents and skills, and placed you in your sphere of influence. You have been given great things, yet you also have great responsibility to be that difference.As you allow God to use you to be a Kingdom leader, I would love to hear from you. Please share your stories with me online at www.taylormorton.net May God bless you as you leverage your impact to make a difference for His kingdom!

Taylor Morton
August 2019

ACKNOWLEDGMENTS

Leadership is something that must be handled delicately and is not something everyone will grasp. Leadership is not about ruling over others, but it is about taking care of those that God has entrusted to you. I am thankful for the many leaders in my life that took time out of their busy lives to invest in me.

To my beautiful wife Linlee, life has not dealt us the easiest hand. You were created for me and I for you. You have been my strength and my rock on my toughest days. You have gone through more than anyone should ever have to experience in this life and you are without a doubt, the strongest person I know. You are also the most selfless person I know. You put others before your every need, and I am so blessed to call you my Proverbs 31 wife.

To Mom, Dad, and T.J, I am so thankful for the bond we have as a family. I am grateful for a Dad who has never wavered in his leadership and always pointed me to Jesus. I am thankful for a Mom who loved me unconditionally and a Mom who made so many sacrifices so that Trent, T.J., and I would never go without. I am also thankful for the bond that I have with my youngest brother, T.J., we have stuck together through it all, and I pray we will continue to do so.

To Mr. David and Grantland, I couldn't have asked for a better father-in-law and brother-in-law. You guys have taken me in as your own, and I am forever grateful for that. To Scott and Brent, thank you for writing the forewords of this book. Both of you have invested so much in me, and I could not be more thankful for your leadership and friendship. You took a chance on me when no one else ever would have given me an opportunity. Thank you for being two of my most significant role models and two men of God that I am continually learning from.

To Dr. Jay Strack, you introduced the idea of leadership and dreaming to me and to hundreds of thousands of other students. In 2009 my Dad took me to SLU 101 in Orlando Florida. You challenged us to ask ourselves the question "what would I do for the glory of God if I knew I wouldn't fail?" I wrote my dream down, and was able to accomplish that dream through the skills you equipped me with through my SLU journey. SLU gave me a twenty-year quantum leap amongst my peers and I am forever grateful for the leadership journey that you ignited in my life. Thank you for being a lifelong mentor and an incredible friend.

To my church family at Valley View, thank you for being the type of church that opens her doors to anyone who would desire to come in. Thank you for not being a museum for the righteous, but a hospital for the broken. Thank you for standing firm on God's word and never wavering from what the word of God speaks to His church. To my pastor, Brother Billy, thank you for being personable and being an approachable pastor. Thank you for investing in me as a leader. I have learned so much in my time at Valley View, and I cannot wait to see what the future has in store. Thank you for being more than a pastor and being an incredible friend. From the countless movies to the lunches at La Gran, I am forever grateful for our friendship.

To my youth staff at Valley View, from my ministry assistant, Jordan, to my interns Will, Trent, and Evan, thank you for fighting the fight with me. We have a generation that we are continually pointing towards the Kingdom. You guys are indeed a God-send, and you are the team that enables the teamwork to make the dream work.

Lastly, to my students at Valley View, and my former students at Centreville and Enon; this book is for you. My heart is to see each one of you pursue and fulfill your God-given dream. My prayer is that this journey would ignite a fire inside of you that would produce and unleash the Kingdom leader within you. That it would produce the Kingdom leader, you were created to be! Thank you for allowing me to be apart of your journey and for allowing me to have a small part in the pursuit of your dreams.

ABOUT THE AUTHOR

Taylor is a thought-provoking leader who engages audiences with humor and stories. Taylor travels the country speaking to churches, athletic teams, and businesses. Taylor's story challenges them to become the best version of themselves they can be.

"Taylor's story is one everyone should hear. It shows what perseverance and faith can do when life presents the greatest challenges."
- Nick Saban
University of Alabama head football coach

Taylor played football at The University of Alabama from 2011-2014. He was apart of two national championships and one SEC championship. While attending the University, he was diagnosed with cancer during his junior year. He is now cancer free and is married to the love of his life Linlee. They have two german shepherds and live in Tuscaloosa, Al.

Taylor serves on staff at Valley View Baptist Church as their student pastor. He has a passion for challenging each student to be the very best leader they can be and to use their talents, gifts, and abilities for the glory of God.

Facebook - Taylor Morton
Instagram - @taylormorton12
Email - info@taylormorton.net

Made in the
USA
Lexington, KY